THE LITTLE BOOK
OF
Unicorns

Published in 2022 by OH!
An Imprint of Welbeck Non-Fiction Limited,
part of Welbeck Publishing Group.
Based in London and Sydney.
www.welbeckpublishing.com

Disclaimer:
This book is intended for general informational purposes only and should not be relied upon as recommending or promoting any specific practice, diet or method of treatment. It is not intended to diagnose, advise, treat or prevent any illness or condition and is not a substitute for advice from a professional practitioner of the subject matter contained in this book. You should not use the information in this book as a substitute for medication, nutritional, diet, spiritual or other treatment that is prescribed by your practitioner. The publisher makes no representations or warranties with respect to the accuracy, completeness or currency of the contents of this work, and specifically disclaim, without limitation, any implied warranties of merchantability or fitness for a particular purpose and any injury, illness, damage, death, liability or loss incurred, directly or indirectly from the use or application of any of the contents of this book. Furthermore, the publisher is not affiliated with and does not sponsor or endorse any uses of or beliefs about in any way referred in this book.

ISBN 978-1-80069-173-5

Compiled and written by: Lisa Dyer
Editorial: Victoria Godden
Project manager: Russell Porter
Design: Emily Clarke
Production: Jess Brisley

A CIP catalogue record for this book is available from the British Library

Printed in China

10 9 8 7 6 5 4 3 2 1

THE LITTLE BOOK
OF
Unicorns

Add some
Sparkling
Unicorn Magic
to your life!

Contents

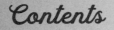

Introduction

*A*dd some sparkling unicorn magic to your life with this empowering guide to unlocking your creativity, courage and optimism. Along with captivating myths and legends, inspirational quotes and positive affirmations, there are spells, rituals, recipes, crystal work, self-care tips and much more, all of which will help you enter the realm of unicorns and live like them – vibrantly, gracefully, resiliently and joyfully.

Uniting strength and mysticism with beauty and kindness, the unicorn was first recorded in the 4th century BCE, and over time has captured human imagination with stories of valour, healing and enchantment. As tales of old would tell, the unicorn could only be lured by the virginal maiden, and so it thus came to symbolize innocence and purity. But the unicorn is much more than that, as you will learn on the following pages; it represents all that is unique, magical and special about each and every one of us.

Here you will find ways to awaken your creativity, face challenges, harness happiness, build confidence and make positive changes in your life and the world. You will be able to strengthen your ability to fight for what you believe in and to say no to the things you don't. You will learn how to move toward your goals, become your best, most authentic self and always dream big, and bigger.

Throughout the book are power affirmations to lift your heart, mind, body and spirit. Just repeating the same life-enhancing words, again and again, can re-train your brain to think differently about the most important things – yourself, your future and your loved ones. There are many brilliant ideas and exercises for self-care, positive thinking and self-love, as well as tips for keeping your body and mind healthy and hopeful... Because sometimes life isn't all unicorns and rainbows, but it can be.

CHAPTER
One

Myth & Magic

Step into the enchanted world
of unicorns and discover their
stories and secrets,
along with some magical spells
and rituals to explore their
potent powers.

"The unicorns were the most *recognizable magic* the fairies possessed, and they sent them to those worlds where belief in the magic was in danger of falling altogether. After all, *there has to be some belief in magic*, however small, for any world to survive."

TERRY BROOKS,
THE BLACK UNICORN (1987)

10

"Wherever they may have come from, and wherever they may have gone, unicorns live inside the true believer's heart. Which means *as long as we can dream, there will be unicorns.* **"**

BRUCE COVILLE,
THE LORE OF THE UNICORN (1987)

Ancient Tales & Sightings

Many of our modern ideas of the unicorn
date from myths, folklore and early recorded sightings
of a unicorn-like creature across many cultures.

🌿 The unicorn appeared earliest in Mesopotamian
art, circa 3000–1300 BCE, notably in the imagery
on seals belonging to the elite in the Indus Valley
civilization.

🌿 In Chinese mythology, the appearance of the unicorn, called the *qilin*, coincides with the births and deaths of sages and emperors, and can fortell the future of an unborn child. It has the body of a deer, the tail of an ox, a yellow belly and multicoloured back.

🌿 The Persian *kardakann* is also a shapeshifter but a terrifying and ferocious warrior with a pure gold horn; it is a threat to all animals except the ring dove, which is the only animal able to tame it.

🌿 Known as *qué ly* or *lan* in Vietnamese folklore, where it decorates temples, this shapeshifting unicorn is sacred and signifies prosperity, good luck, long life and happiness.

🌿 In Japanese mythology there are two unicorns: the Sin-You is judgemental and can detect lies (it is said to able to pierce the heart of a liar), while the Kirin is shy and gentle.

🌿 In India, the unicorn creature *rysa* has a human counterpart called Rsyasrnga who also sports a horn in the middle of his forehead.

🌿 The earliest description of unicorns in Greek literature was by the historian Ctesias, who related that a single-horned (Greek *monokers*, Latin *unicornis*) animal was the size of a horse and very like an oryx.

🌿 In the early Christian era, the unicorn was
  believed to be savage, in part due to Ctesias'
  descriptions of its ferocity and swiftness.
  Hunters couldn't capture a unicorn; it could only
  be tamed by a virgin maiden – the unicorn
  would rest in her lap,
  enabling him to
  be restrained.

🌿 In the Bible, a strong and splendid horned animal called re'em, one translation of which is 'unicorn'. Allegorically, it was a strong fierce animal likened to Christ, which is why only pure maids, such as the Virgin Mary, could tame them.

🌿 Pliny the Elder, in first century CE, writes of the monokeros or "single horn" having the "head of the stag, the feet of the elephant, and the tail of the boar, while the rest of the body is like that of the horse" with a single black horn (suspiciously like a rhino!). He stated they were the most ferocious of animals in India and impossible to capture alive.

🌿 Julius Caesar, circa 50 BCE, recorded a tall stag with a single horn living in the ancient and dense Hercynian Forest of Germany.

🌿 In 6th century CE, a travelling Egyptian merchant, Cosmas Indicopleustes, tells of the unicorn's power resting in his horn; when in danger, the animal would plunge over a cliff to escape, safely landing on the point of his horn.

🌿 Associated with chivalry and virtue in medieval
Europe, the unicorn is famously depicted in the
Hunt of the Unicorn tapestries – a series of
seven scenes showing hunters capturing a unicorn
– created circa 1500. In one tapestry a snake
has poisoned a pool of water in the forest and a
unicorn is dipping in his horn to purify it.

🌿 By the 15th century, the unicorn starts appearing
in heraldry, symbolizing purity and power, often
depicted with a broken chain around its neck.

🌿 The scientific consensus of the 1800s was that assorted land animals, including the elusive unicorn, had yet to be discovered or fully understood; this view was underpinned by the writings of philosopher and scientist Gottfried Leibniz in Protogaea (1749) and his sketch of a unicorn skeleton found in 1663.

🌿 One scientific theory says the unicorn existed as the Siberian unicorn, *Elasmotherium sibiricum*, a type of rhinoceros that lived in the Eurasian steppes which became extinct in the Ice Age.

THE Noah's Ark LEGEND

According to legend, the unicorns were late arriving to Noah's Ark because they were busy playing in the woods, so Noah had to tie them to the ark by their horns and drag them along behind, during which time they transformed into the flesh-and-blood narwhal. This is why many believe the narwhal's spiral tusk to be the unicorn's horn.

THE
Garden of Eden
STORY

In one biblical tale, Adam named the unicorn before any other animal. When he and Eve left the Garden of Eden, the unicorn went with them because it was so loyal. However, unlike Adam and Eve, the unicorn could return to the Garden every century. By eating the vegetation and drinking the water, it renewed its strength. As the unicorn belongs to the angelic realm, it could be thought of as the humans' guardian angel.

Where to Find Unicorns

In ancient China, all supernatural creatures including unicorns were thought to live in the Mystical Mountains, known as the Shen Shan; in Korea, where the unicorn is known as the *kiringul*, it lives in high mountain caves that contain lakes and fountains of clear water.

In ancient Greece, Ctesias reported seeing unicorns in the Palace of the Forty Pillars in Persepolis, as all supernatural creatures were then thought to live in what were considered magical lands; that is, the Asian continent. In the Middle Ages, the ever-elusive unicorn was thought to reside in the deepest darkest forests, near streams of crystal-clear water.

"This is the violet hour, *the hour of hush and wonder*, when the affections glow and valour is reborn, when the *shadows deepen* along the edge of the forest and we believe that, *if we watch carefully, at any moment we may see the unicorn.*"

BERNARD DEVOTO,
THE HOUR: A COCKTAIL MANIFESTO (1948)

SAY HELLO TO YOUR
Spirit Animal

Your unicorn spirit guide encourages you to free your inner child, be your unique self, open up to wonder and magic and to keep dreaming. This visualization will help when you are feeling pessimistic and world-weary.

Find a quiet place, sit still on the floor on a cushion or outside in a garden. Take a few deep breaths to centre yourself. When you feel ready, envision your unicorn guide coming to you and kneeling before you. Look into its eyes and hold out your hand, inviting it to nuzzle. If you feel it is right, invite it to put its head in your lap.

LET THE UNICORN'S PEACE AND POSITIVITY WASH OVER YOU.

Spell to Summon a Unicorn

Align with the unicorn virtues and encourage contact with your unicorn spirit with this spell.

★ White linen cloth
★ Fresh flower, either a white rose, orchid or a purple lilac
★ White candle
★ White quartz or lepidolite crystal
★ Offerings, such as apples, berries, oats or a cinnamon stick
★ Lavender or lilac essential oil and oil burner, or incense

Make an altar by placing the cloth on a flat surface. Arrange the flower, candle, crystal and any offerings on the cloth. Set up the oil burner or incense. Light the candle and the oil burner or incense. Sit quietly and envision a wise, noble and beautiful unicorn. Connect to its purity and power.

Keep Your Unicorn Close

A great way to remind yourself of the unicorn's magic and optimism and imbue that spirit into your daily life is to carry around a token, symbol or figure. Place items in a coat pocket, on a shelf where you work or cook, beside your bed, or throughout the house where you can see them. Here are some suggestions:

★ A wearable unicorn image (on a T-shirt, piece of jewellery or hair ornament)
★ Picture or painting of a unicorn
★ Statue or figurine
★ Ribbons in pastel or rainbow colours
★ Unicorn stickers

'Do you know, I always thought unicorns were fabulous monsters, too? I never saw one alive before!'

'Well, now that we have seen each other,' said the unicorn, 'if you'll believe in me, I'll believe in you.'

LEWIS CARROLL'S
THROUGH THE LOOKING-GLASS (1871)

Wish Upon a Unicorn

Unicorns can grant wishes, but they
will only do so for unselfish ones.
This spell should be performed outside
in the moonlight under a tree or near a
water source, such as a fountain, pool,
pond or stream.

★ Apple
★ Sparkling water or wine

Sit quietly by the base of the tree or by the water.
Address the unicorn aloud, politely explaining that
you are asking for its help in granting your wish.
Speak your wish, thank the unicorn, then decant the
water or wine at the roots of the tree or on the
water bank. Leave the apple as an offering. Even if the
unicorn won't grant your wish, you must still express
gratitude that it took the time to listen.

Virtues & Powers

Here are a few of the many virtues associated with this magical beast:

MAGIC: Able to bestow wisdom, wishes and miracles on the virtuous, the unicorn can mesmerize and enchant. Its horn is thought to act like a wizard's wand and cast magic.

LIGHT and **INSIGHT:**

A creature of light, the unicorn symbolizes deep knowledge and understanding.

STRENGTH:

Ferocious in fighting, fleet of hoof, fearless and a heroic warrior, the unicorn is often considered deceptively fierce and deadly.

TRANSCENDENCE:

Associated with both femininity (the moon) and the masculine (the horn), the unicorn unites and transcends gender.

HEALING:
The spiral horn and the mane of the unicorn especially are thought to possess healing powers and offer good fortune.

LOYALTY:
A devoted and loyal defender of the innocent and champion of the underdog, the unicorn is also associated with faithfulness – if lovers spot a unicorn they will have everlasting love.

INNOCENCE:
Only the most pure of heart can see the unicorn, and it is tamed only in the arms of a virgin woman.

FREEDOM and **TRAVEL:**

Unicorns are the fastest creatures as they can move across space and time. As they gallop through all dimensions and realms and can appear in any time and place they wish, they symbolize travel, adventure and freedom.

Unicorn Tears

Tears wept by the unicorn are rare and elusive; once it sheds a tear the animal dies within the hour. Because of this, "unicorn tears" has come to mean anything rare, magical and valuable. They are also said to have the ability to heal the body and cure a broken heart.

Healing Heart Tea

Drink this tea to help let go of love and heal heartbreak.

★ 1 tsp dried red clover
★ 1 tsp dried rosebuds
★ 1 tsp raspberry leaf
★ 400 ml (1½ cups) filtered water

Place the red clover, rose and raspberry in a teapot. Boil the water in a kettle and pour over the ingredients. Cover and allow to steep for 5 to 10 minutes. Drink the tea, concentrating on positive thoughts of future love to come.

Unicorn Hair

Extremely potent, hair from the mane and tail of the unicorn is said to have been used in magical potions, medicines, spells and in the construction of wizards' wands.

If woven, unicorn hair is thought to make any cloth indestructible.

Unicorn Blood

Like unicorn tears, the blood is believed to cure wounds and injuries.

Able to save life if consumed, it comes at a cost, as whoever slays a unicorn is cursed for eternity! The life that is saved is said to be a zombie-like "half-life".

Moon Manifestation Magic

This practice will create a sacred space for you to focus inwards, spread goodwill and take time to decide what your needs are for life on earth. Ideally, do this at the full moon, when you can clearly see the moonlight and stand in its path.

★ White candle
★ Matches or lighter
★ Pen and paper
★ Glass jar or box

Go outside in moonlight or set yourself up in a room where you can see the moon shining through the window.

Light the candle and ask the unicorn to watch over you for safety and protection. Write all the things you would like to happen in the month ahead on the paper. Fold the paper and place it in the jar or box in the moonlight. Stay there for 15 minutes meditating quietly on your intentions.

In the morning, bring the jar or box inside and place the list where you can see it daily.

"The moon was gone, but to the magician's eyes *the unicorn was the moon*, cold and white and very old, lighting his way to safety, or to madness."

PETER S. BEAGLE,
THE LAST UNICORN (1968)

39

Unicorn Horn

In the Middle Ages, cups made of unicorn horn (also called alicorn and thought now to be rhino or narwhal tusk) were valued as a protection against poisoned drinks and disease. Fragments of horn, called *touches* by the French and sometimes worn in a chain around the neck, could be touched or dipped into plates of food to detect the presence of toxins. If the horn turned colour, produced condensation or steam, or made the drink bubble, a poison was present.

Powdered horn was often added to potions and medicines and used to treat dog bites, wounds, plague, gout, measles, fever, pain and leprosy, and as an aphrodisiac.

Test the Waters

How to tell if you are in possession of a true unicorn horn? Do as the medieval folk did and place three spiders inside and cover the top. If the spiders die, the horn is real.

Royal Treasures

Queen Elizabeth I was given a fully intact horn by explorer Martin Frobisher that she used as a sceptre and which became known as the Horn of Windsor. It was valued at £10,000, about £2 million today. Magical unicorn horns were popular as state gifts. Philip II of Spain apparently had 12 and, in the late 1600s, Christian V of Denmark sat on a throne of unicorn horns, which was used in ceremonies for centuries afterwards.

THE STORY OF
King John I

King John I of Aragon (1350–1396) loved hunting and was also interested in astrology and alchemy. Suffering from epilepsy, he sought a unicorn horn for a cure. The Count of Armagnac sent him a piece of unicorn horn and the king tested it by poisoning two dogs, then touching just one with the horn. The one who was touched lived, the other died, and the king went on to cure other subjects who had been poisoned.

Energy Purification

To clear and balance the energy around you, perform this purification ritual. It will cleanse the space of negativity and usher in positivity. You may like to do this in a room, your whole house, an office or a bedroom before you sleep.

★ White sage smudge stick
★ Small hand brush or besom (optional)
★ Matches or lighter
★ Small glass bowl

Before you begin, think of an intention, such as "I release all toxic energy" or "I welcome only positive energy here", and keep this in mind as you perform the ritual.

Open all the windows and doors, light the smudge stick and, once it is burning well, blow out the flame to leave it smoking.

Walking clockwise around the room, use the besom or your hand to waft the plumes of smoke into every area and corner of the room, focusing your intention all the while.

When you are finished, place the smudge stick in the bowl and allow it to extinguish.
* Never leave a burning stick or flame unattended.

CHAPTER

Two

Unicorn Power

Recharge your inner unicorn
and build up your physical
and mental strength with these
healing remedies, health and
exercise tips and sleep advice, as
well as some simple drink
and snack recipes.

"The unicorn was a marvellous beast, shining with **HONOUR**, *wisdom* and **STRENGTH**. Just to see him strengthened the soul.**"**

MEGAN LINDHOLM,
*"THE UNICORN IN THE MAZE", THE
UNICORN TREASURY* (2004)

What would life be
if we had no
COURAGE
to attempt
anything?

VINCENT VAN GOGH

AFFIRMATION:
I am a
Freakin' Fierce Unicorn

My mind is a powerful thing.
When I fill it with positive
thoughts, I can rise to any
challenge that comes
my way.

Live Courageously

Welcoming challenges can be hard for even the most robust unicorn, but you can learn to live more boldly and bravely by demonstrating your courage. Take the time to help a person who is in distress or in a challenging situation. Instead of ignoring them or the problem, call for help or step in and take charge.

Whip Up That Willpower

Feeling uninspired or just plain bored? Here are some tips for rustling up that unicorn energy to reach your objectives, whether it's better health, fitness and diet or education, career and life goals.

1. BELIEVE!
Science has proven that exercising willpower can generate more of it, so tell yourself you have a limitless supply of self-discipline, and you will.

2. SET GOALS.

Thinking of the finishing line and
imagining how great you will feel
helps when you're flagging.

3. FOCUS ON THE SMALL STEPS.

If you are getting overwhelmed, break
it down into smaller, easier-to-achieve
goals and set a reward, such as a
special coffee or a massage, when
you reach each one.

4. PLAN FOR SCREWING UP.

Think about what triggers you have that could derail you, and prepare for how you are going to deal with them if and when they surface.

5. KEEP FORWARD MOTION.

Staying busy and active will help maintain the momentum.

6. MAINTAIN THE MACHINE.
Your body needs good fuel,
exercise and sleep to keep the
gears oiled and working efficiently!
Don't run on empty.

7. TAKE A BREAK.
Listen to music, do yoga or meditation,
read a book, draw, write in your journal
– anything that will help you avoid
stress, burnout and giving up.

8. CHOOSE YOUR INFLUENCERS.

Hang out with like-minded people and lean on your friends and loved ones for support. If you regularly keep in touch with them, it will help avoid a crisis point or meltdown, and even if that happens, they will be on hand.

9. AVOID TEMPTATIONS.

Keep only healthy food in the
house, delete your takeaway app,
opt for a walk in the park
with friends instead of meeting
for a drink.

10. DON'T
GO DOWN THE
RABBIT HOLE.

Limit your social media
usage to set times of
the day.

Apothecary Medicine

English botanist Nicholas Culpeper (1616–1654) advocated the use of powdered unicorn horn in medicines, especially those to restore vitality. It was such a popular ingredient that the Worshipful Society of Apothecaries, founded in 1617, features unicorns on its crest.

Under the Weather?

Even unicorns can get sick. Their sparkles fade, their mane and tail look dull, their fur greys and they lose their pep. If this has happened to you, try these tricks.

★ Drink a shot of apple cider vinegar (with the "mother") in the morning.

★ Eat small light meals frequently throughout the day or try a one-day cold-pressed juice fast.

★ Cut out all caffeine, alcohol, dairy and meat until you feel better.

★ Drink a night-time tea of passionflower or chamomile and go to bed early.

Herbal Remedies

The famed herbalist Hildegard of Bingen believed unicorn liver, mixed with egg yolks, could cure leprosy. She also believed wearing a belt of unicorn hide would save you from pestilence. In *Liber Physica* she wrote: "The unicorn is more hot than cold. Its strength is greater than its heat. It eats clean plants... it avoids a man but follows a woman."

Unicorn Herbs & Spices

Use these herbs and roots in your food or as infusions in teas or tinctures to stimulate self-healing. Many of them are also available in essential oil form for use in mood-enhancing beauty products, room sprays and fragrances.

- 🌿 For Strength: Ashwagandha, basil, St John's wort, turmeric.

- 🌿 For Healing: Echinacea, evening primrose, feverfew, milk thistle, nettle.

- 🌿 For Energy: Ginseng, rosemary, peppermint, sage.

- 🌿 For Sleep: Chamomile, lavender, passionflower, valerian root.

Enchanted Sleep

All unicorns know you can't work and play
without rest. To get your sleeping beauty slumber,
follow these tips.

★ Unplug your digital devices.

★ Drink a herbal tea or milky golden turmeric latte.

★ Go to bed at the same time each night and
perform the same pre-bed rituals.

★ Practise meditation to still an active mind.

★ Keep your bedroom on the cool side, at about
15.6-18°C (60-65°F).

★ Use a pillow mist spray, an eye mask and earplugs.

Return to Dreamland

Don't let disturbed nights affect your brave, strong, resilient inner unicorn! Try these tricks to get back to sleep fast.

★ Breathe deeply. Try the 4:7:8 method where you inhale through your nose for a count of 4, hold for a count of 7 and exhale through your mouth for a count of 8.

★ Count backwards from 100.

★ Practise muscle relaxation. Starting at your toes, and working up toward your head, focus on relaxing each body part before moving on to the next.

★ Keep a sleep diary. This can help you identify any recurring problems.

Leap Like a Unicorn

There may be no gyms in the enchanted forest, but luckily we have them here. The unicorn likes the open air, so try to get outside for your exercise.

RUNNING: Super-fast sprints are much better for fat burning, heart health, muscle building and metabolism than slower long runs.

STRENGTH TRAINING: Builds muscle, supports joints and increases bone density.

YOGA: Increases strength, balance and flexibility, while being both energizing and relaxing. This is the ideal unicorn exercise.

CLIMBING AND HILL WALKING: Works a wide range of muscle groups, aids in mental focus and awareness, plus it connects you with nature.

DANCE: Builds strength, helps the heart and lungs, increases aerobic fitness and endurance.

Unicorn Dance Party

A symbol of power and prosperity, the Vietnamese
perform the unicorn dance on special occasions
such as New Year's Eve as part of their
Tet festival, but in true unicorn form,
practise your own freestyle dance
moves to get some exercise.
Try a Zumba class or check
out TikTok for inspiration
and start a kitchen disco.

YOGA THE *Unicorn* WAY

Of course unicorns practise yoga. The most agile creatures on the earth are obviously bendy too! Here are their specialities.

CRESCENT LUNGE: From a standing position, step your right foot forward into a lunge with your knee directly over your right ankle. Inhale and raise both arms straight up above your head like the unicorn horn.

Lift your heart, look up and hold for a few deep breaths. Switch sides and repeat.

SPARKLING STAR POSE: From a standing position, step your feet out wide. Stretch both arms out to the sides and above the head, with your fingers spread out as wide as you can. Reach to the universe and hold for 10 deep breaths.

RAINBOW BRIDGE: Lie on your back with your knees bent, your feet flat and heels below your knees. Your arms should lie flat along your sides. Press your elbows to the ground, lift your chest and tuck in your shoulder blades.

On an inhale, lift your buttocks to create a rainbow curve and clasp your hands under you. Hold for five deep breaths.

Walk in the Sunlight

Unicorns need sunlight (and moonlight!) not only because it is their main source of energy, but for vigour, all-round health and that positive frame of mind. Follow your magical friend and make sure you get your daily dose by taking a walk outside.

AFFIRMATION:
Healing Light

A unicorn beam of brilliant light fills my
heart and radiates through me. Let this
light spark every atom of my body,
purifying and energizing me and
touching everyone I meet as
I go about my day. I
radiate light.

Outdoor Activities for Unicorns

🍃 Get daily exercise with lots of fresh air.

🍃 Take frequent visits to forests and ancient woodlands – make sure you do a bit of tree-hugging and forest-bathing!

🍃 Go to fresh water sources – lakes, babbling brooks and waterfalls will awaken your unicorn energy.

🍃 Eat al fresco whenever you can and take picnics to local beauty spots.

❧ Explore caves and spring-fed grottos; these were considered portals between earthly and spiritual worlds and the home of gods in ancient times.

❧ Pick wildflowers in meadows, make daisy chains and forage for fruit, mushrooms and herbs.

❧ Grow a vegetable patch and herb garden, or plant a tree, if you have space in your garden.

❧ Camp under the stars or rent a stargazing pod.

71

Healthy Snacks

As herbivores, unicorns love to load up on fresh fruit and vegetables (they can't live on a diet of rainbows alone!). Here are some human equivalents.

★ **NUTS** and **SEEDS** contain the perfect balance of healthy fats, protein and fibre and provide a boost of energy.

★ **APPLE SLICES** with **PEANUT BUTTER** – both are rich in antioxidants that help gut health and the heart.

★ **AVOCADO DIP** with **RAW VEGGIES** – avocados are high in healthy fats, fibre, potassium and magnesium.

★ **EDAMAME** is high in protein, keeping you full for longer, as well as folate, iron, magnesium and manganese.

RAINBOW POPCORN

½ cup **CASTER SUGAR** (superfine)
2 tbsp water
1 drop each of blue, red, purple and green
    FOOD COLOURING
8 cups plain air-popped **POPCORN**

Line 4 baking trays with parchment paper.
In a medium saucepan, combine the sugar and water
to make sugar syrup. Heat gently, stirring, until the
sugar has dissolved, then increase the heat for five
more minutes and stir until it has reduced to a syrup.

Add one-quarter of the sugar syrup to a bowl, stir
in a drop of blue food colouring, then add 2 cups of
popcorn, stirring to coat. Spread out on the baking
tray to cool.

Repeat with the remaining sugar syrup and food
colouring.

UNICORN TOAST

250g (8oz) **CREAM CHEESE**, softened
3 tsp **HONEY**
1 drop each pink, purple, yellow, green and blue **FOOD COLOURING**
4 slices **BREAD**, toasted,. or 2 sliced **BAGELS**, toasted
Pastel-coloured **SPRINKLES**, edible glitter, gold leaf or **POPPING CANDY**, to top

Mix the cream cheese and honey together until smooth, then divide between five small bowls.

Add 1 drop of food colouring to each bowl, stir and adjust colouring if required.

Swirl a little of each colour over each toast or bagel slice, alternating the colours, then top with sprinkles, glitter, gold or popping candy.

BLUE UNICORN SMOOTHIE BOWL

2 large frozen **BANANAS**, chopped
¼ cup **COCONUT MILK**
½ tsp blue **SPIRULINA** powder
Juice from ½ **LEMON**
2 tbsp **COCONUT MILK POWDER**
BLUEBERRIES, **RASPBERRIES**, **COCONUT YOGURT** and
   COCONUT FLAKES, to top

Combine all the ingredients except the toppings in
a blender until smooth. Add a little more coconut
milk if needed.

Pour into a bowl and add the toppings.

HYDRO-BOOSTING FRUIT INFUSION

★ Assorted **FRUIT**: blueberries, strawberries, raspberries, kiwi, peach and mango
★ Wide-mouthed **GLASS BOTTLES WITH LIDS**
★ Sparkling or still filtered water
★ **PAPER STRAWS**

Prepare the fruit by cleaning, peeling and hulling as necessary and then chop the fruit into bite-sized chunks. Keep the blueberries whole.

Drop the fruit in coloured layers – first blue fruits, then red, then green, and finally the peach and mango – into each glass bottle. Top up with sparkling or still water. Screw on the lids and leave to infuse for 10 minutes before serving with straws.

Keep refilling with water throughout the day; or drain and eat as a fruit salad!

Magical Moon Water

Make some moon-charged water by placing a crystal glass or goblet of water under the light of the full moon and allow it to charge overnight, then drink it down at dawn!

* To manifest a desire, write your intention in a letter, fold it and place it under the glass before leaving it in the moonlight. By consuming the water the next morning, you will be absorbing the intention.

UNICORN LEMONADE

1 cup water
3 silicone **ICE-CUBE TRAYS**
Blue, pink and purple **FOOD COLOURING**
Sparkling **LEMONADE**
LEMON slices and **MINT** sprigs

Add 1 cup of water to a measuring
jug and stir in 2 drops of blue
food colouring. Pour the blue
water into an ice-cube tray.
Repeat with the remaining food
colours to make up the other
trays. Place in the freezer for 4–6
hours until frozen.

When frozen, add ice cubes in each colour
to a glass and top up with lemonade.
Garnish with the lemon "wheel" and mint.

GLITTER ICE CUBES

Silicone **ICE-CUBE TRAYS**
EDIBLE GLITTER in silver and pastel colours
  of your choice

Place about ¼ teaspoon of glitter in the base of
each cube then half-fill with hot water (this will help
make the ice look crystal clear).

Place in the freezer for 4-6 hours until frozen. The
glitter will float to the top of the cube.

* If you want imbedded glitter, top the cubes up with
more water and place the trays back in the freezer.

UNICORN SMOOTHIE

10 **STRAWBERRIES**, cleaned and hulled
1 frozen **BANANA**
¼ cup **ORANGE JUICE**
ALMOND MILK, as needed

Drizzle:
1 tablespoon **RAW CASHEW BUTTER**
¼ teaspoon **BLUE SPIRULINA POWDER** or **MATCHA**
½ cup **GREEK YOGURT**
1 tablespoon water

Toppings:
COCONUT WHIPPED CREAM
FREEZE-DRIED STRAWBERRY or **BLUEBERRY** powder
Mini **MARSHMALLOWS**

Stir together the drizzle ingredients and place in a piping bag. Keep chilled while you prepare the smoothie.

Combine the main ingredients together in a blender, adding almond milk until you get the consistency you desire.

In a tall glass, pipe the drizzle in a swirl around the inside of the glass. Fill the glass with the smoothie. Top with whipped cream, more drizzle, berry powder and marshmallows.

SPARKLY UNICORN TOPPINGS

Here are some of the extras you can add to sweet and savoury food and hot and cold drinks to give them that unicorn sparkle. Choose gold, silver, pastels, rainbow colours and those labelled as unicorn or mermaid mixes.

- ★ **WHIPPED CREAM** – add a few different drops of food colouring and swirl through for a marbled effect.
- ★ **EDIBLE GLITTER**, **SPRINKLES** and star confetti
- ★ **POPPING CANDY** in fruit flavours
- ★ Sparkling **SUGAR CRYSTALS**, pearls, dust and candyfloss sugar
- ★ **MINI MARSHMALLOWS** in pink and white
- ★ Edible **GOLD** and **SILVER LEAF**
- ★ **SPARKLE DROPS** are available in various flavours to colour and flavour beverages

Sprinkle Mix

Make your own DIY unicorn sprinkles by mixing together white and silver hundreds-and-thousands with pastel sprinkles, confetti stars, nonpareils and sequin sprinkles.
Keep in a jar and use to decorate food.

Flower Food

Add fresh edible flowers to salads, desserts and drinks. Choose from nasturtium, borage, rose, lavender, violet, dandelion and honeysuckle.

CHAPTER
Three

Unicorn Beauty

Celebrate all the uniqueness
that is you with these tips
for physical self-care, from body
positivity and inner beauty
to treatments for the hair, skin
and nails.

BE A UNICORN IN A FIELD FULL OF HORSES.

ANONYMOUS

"Be a *diamond-studded* unicorn: UNBREAKABLE and *unique*."

COCO,
UNICORN PSYCHOSIS: A POETIC JOURNEY
(2019)

Embrace Your Uniqueness

One person is beautiful in one way, and another in some other way. And that's how it should be!

CAN YOU IMAGINE IF WE WERE ALL THE SAME INSTEAD OF BEING THE UNIQUE, SPECIAL AND RARE UNICORNS WE ARE?

You are meant to look exactly like you, so stop comparing yourself to others! Write a list of everything you like about yourself and read it whenever doubts creep in.

"Unicorns are **IMMORTAL**. It is their nature to live alone in one place: usually a forest where there is a pool clear enough for them to see themselves – for they are a little vain, *knowing themselves to be the most beautiful.*"

PETER S. BEAGLE,
THE LAST UNICORN (1968)

Inner Beauty

You are so much more than how you look! Think more about the things that you enjoy than what you look like. Throw yourself into your passions. Pick up a new hobby. Take an art class. Catch a coffee with a friend. Your body is a tool for you to use, so use it! You'll appreciate it so much more.

Release Your Inhibitions

Only *you can free yourself* from your concerns, fears and self-judgement. Don't be afraid to **SPEAK UP**, say what you're **FEELING** and give your *opinion*.

Even if no one agrees with you, you have a right to share your journey and experiences. The more you learn to *let go of the fear* of looking foolish or stupid, or being weird or strange, the more you're EMBRACING YOUR INDIVIDUALITY.

Rainbow Manes and Red Horns

Although most depictions of the unicorn are of an angelic white horse-like being with a spiral horn in the forehead often with a rainbow mane and tail, Ctesias described the unicorn, circa 400 BCE, as the size of a horse, with a white body, purple head and blue eyes, and a 45.7 cm (18 inch) horn in its forehead that was coloured red at the pointed tip, black in the middle and white at the base.

92

Express Your Individuality

BE LIKE THE UNICORN: Own your version of beauty and flaunt it. In style and fashion as well as personality, be authentic to you. **TRUST WHAT YOU LIKE AND WHO YOU ARE.**

If your thing is **ECCENTRIC** and **BOLD**, go for it; if you like being on the downlow, that's cool too. If you aren't sure what you like, experiment and try everything once – you'll soon figure it out.

You Are Beautiful

Unicorns don't doubt themselves and neither should you. Here are some ways to practise a little more self-love when it comes to the way you look.

1. BE VOCAL. Compliment yourself and others freely.

2. AVOID NEGATIVE MESSAGES ABOUT THE BODY on social media and advertising. Instead, surround yourself with role models that reinforce a positive body image.

3. WATCH YOUR SELF–TALK. Speak to yourself as you would to a good friend. Be encouraging, supportive, excited and positive. Any time a negative thought pops in your head, immediately replace it with a positive one.

4. FOCUS ON HEALTH, NOT WEIGHT. Exercise and a good diet should not be a punishment; it should be fun and make you feel good. Embrace it!

5. RESPECT YOUR BODY. Don't overwork your body or ignore it when it's hungry, tired or emotional.

Skincare Tips.

DO

★ Know your skin type and use the correct cleanser and moisturizer, day and night.

★ Hydrate. It's basic but it works. Drink lots of water and make sure you eat food with a high water content, such as celery and watermelon.

★ Use a daily sunscreen of at least SPF30.

★ Remove your makeup before bed.

DON'T

★ Use too many products or swap them too often. There is no need, ever, for a 10- or 17-step regime.

★ Touch your face. On average we do this 23 times an hour and it can cause breakouts and spread viruses.

★ Neglect your throat and decolletage areas.

★ Skimp on sleep. Your skin needs the night hours to repair the day's cellular damage.

HYDRATING ROSEWATER FACE MIST

Calming and soothing, this mist can be used as a moisturizing treat (or a toner if you add a tablespoon of witch hazel) after cleansing or as a great way to cool down in hot weather.

- ★ 1½ cups **DISTILLED WATER**
- ★ ½ cup fresh **ROSE PETALS** or ¼ cup dried rose petals
- ★ Small saucepan
- ★ Glass spray bottle or atomizer
- ★ 2-3 drops **ROSE ESSENTIAL OIL**

Place the water and rose petals in the pan and simmer for 15 minutes until the colour has washed from the petals. Let cool, strain and decant into the bottle.

Add the rose essential oil and shake gently.
Store for up to a week in the refrigerator.

* Ready-bought rosewater can be used
  too – the effects will be stronger
  than your home-made version.

AFFIRMATION:
Happy Body
Happy Mind

When I eat well, exercise, take care
of my body and get enough sleep,
I am investing in myself and my
mental health.

97

Hand Care Tips

Keep your hooves smooth and beautiful by following these dos and don'ts.

DO

★ Use a moisturizing cream hand wash – the clear versions are usually alcohol-based and drying.

★ If using a hand sanitizer, follow up with a heavy moisturizing cream.

★ Slather on an easily absorbable oil-based hand cream before bed every night, or use an overnight hand mask.

★ Exfoliate hands at bath-time, paying particular attention to the cuticles.

★ Wear gloves to do household tasks.

DON'T

★ Expose your hands to very hot or very cold water, which can cause dryness or redness.

★ Pry open items using your nails.

★ Peel off your polish.

★ Use cuticle trimmers, metal files or metal cuticle pushers that can damage the nail bed and surface.

★ File back-and-forth. File in one direction only!

STICKER UNICORN NAILS

Decals are an easy way to embellish your
nails and you can buy packs that include rainbows,
unicorns, flowers and clouds.

★ Clear base coat
★ **SILVER** nail polish
★ Silver **GLITTER POLISH**
★ Self-adhesive **UNICORN** nail decals
★ Clear topcoat

Apply the clear base coat.
Apply one coat of silver polish.
Top with one coat of silver glitter polish.

When fully dry, stick a different decal onto each nail.
Finish with a clear topcoat to seal. Allow to dry.

* Alternatively, apply two coats of 3D holographic
pearlized nail polish for steps 2 and 3.

GLITTER DUST NAILS

This technique uses a rubber latex base coat, which avoids the use of nail polish remover. You can really build up the glitter this way without worrying about damage.

★ Latex peel-off base coat
★ **PINK** or lilac nail polish
★ Small makeup **SPONGE**
★ **SPARKLING GLITTER** dust powder, such as unicorn or chrome

Apply the latex base coat and allow to dry. Apply one coat of the pink or lilac nail polish and allow to dry. Add a second coat, but while still tacky, apply the glitter dust. To do this, dip the small makeup sponge into the dust or use your finger and dab the glitter onto the nail, pressing in until you build the desired layer. Rub in lightly to buff.

* Use peel-off liquid latex on the surrounding skin to protect cuticles and avoid glitter sticking to the skin.

How to Remove Glitter from Nails

Soak cotton balls in nail polish remover and rest them on each nail. Wrap each one with aluminium foil and leave for 10 minutes to loosen the polish. Then remove the foil, press the cotton pad down and swipe away from the base of the nail.

* Always use a base coat before any nail polish and especially any glitter!

Removing Stains

Usually the stains are only on the topmost layer of the nail so buff the surface with a fine-grit nail buff. Work gently to avoid overbuffing.

Then scrub your nails with a soft toothbrush and a solution of lemon juice and baking soda to clean any remaining stains. Massage cuticle oil all over the nails.

Haircare Tips

Keep your mane strong and healthy by following these dos and don'ts.

DO

★ Apply conditioner to the mid length and ends only and use a weekly overnight mask.

★ Pre-shampoo massage your scalp with coconut or almond oil to boost growth, condition and shine.

★ Detangle with a wide-tooth comb.

★ Use a heat-protection treatment if you are blowdrying or using appliances.

★ Get regular maintenance trims.

DON'T

★ Use products with chemicals; avoid any containing sulphates and parabens.

★ Rub hair dry; instead use a soft T-shirt rather than a bath towel.

★ Swim in chlorinated pools or in seawater without wearing a bathing cap.

★ Over-wash. Daily shampooing can strip hair and is especially damaging for coloured, bleached, chemically treated, dry or porous hair.

★ Brush from the roots. Brush from the ends up to avoid tugging through knots.

Unicorn Hair Colour

You don't need to permanently colour your hair pink and blue to get fun unicorn effects. Try the spray-on and wash-out colours or choose a semi-permanent dye that will last 8-10 washes. Be aware that most work best with light-coloured or bleached hair. Always read the instructions, and to protect skin from colour, make sure you wear gloves and add a layer of petroleum jelly around the hairline.

If you are using a permanent colour, visit a salon to ensure you get professional results. For fun without the commitment, try clip-in extensions or braids in rainbow and pastel colours. Add some ribbons if you want that My Little Pony look!

"Imperfection is *beauty*, madness is **GENIUS** and it's better to be ABSOLUTELY RIDICULOUS than **ABSOLUTELY BORING.**"

MARILYN MONROE,
MARILYN MONROE: IN HER OWN WORDS (1983)

Rose Gold Body Shimmer Oil

Although you can buy ready-made shimmers, here's the chance to customize your body glitter to suit you. Choose the finest glitter you can find. The rose gold suits fairer skins, while gold or bronze is best for darker complexions.

- ★ Glass or recyclable cosmetic bottle
- ★ 1 tsp **ROSE GOLD METALLIC** mica powder or eyeshadow
- ★ Funnel
- ★ Fractionated **COCONUT OIL** or a carrier oil such as almond, jojoba or vitamin E
- ★ Superfine **ROSE GOLD GLITTER**

Take the lid off the bottle and pour in the mica powder.

Using the funnel, decant the oil into the bottle to two-thirds full. Put on the lid and shake well.

Now add the glitter – how much depends on the level of sparkliness you want! Replace the lid and shake well.

AFFIRMATION:
I Celebrate
My Uniqueness

There is no one else in the world like me. I am special and unique and not afraid to be different.

That is my magic.

UNICORN BLEND

Use this combination of essential oils in diffusers or oil burners for a magical room fragrance.

6 drops **FRANKINCENSE** essential oil
6 drops **ORANGE** essential oil
4 drops **ROSE** essential oil
4 drops **BERGAMOT** essential oil
4 drops **MYRRH** essential oil
Small **DROPPER BOTTLE**

Add all the oils to a small clean dropper bottle and store in a cool, dark place.

* Alternatively, combine the essential oils with distilled water and a little vodka or witch hazel in an atomizer to make a perfume spray.

FIZZY ENERGIZING BATH

For sore muscles and fatigue, this zingy bath will relieve aches and pains and restore vitality and energy. You'll be bouncing around like a baby unicorn in no time!

1 cup **BICARBONATE OF SODA** (baking soda)
2 cups **HIMALAYAN EPSOM SALTS**
½ cup **CITRIC ACID**
½ cup **CORNSTARCH**
1 tbsp fractionated **COCONUT OIL**
10 drops each of **ORANGE**, **LEMON**, **PEPPERMINT** essential oils
Large **GLASS JAR** with a screw-top lid

Mix the dry ingredients together in a bowl then slowly add the coconut oil and essential oils, mixing gently. Transfer to the glass jar and keep sealed until use. Use about ½ cup per bath..

COSMIC ESSENTIAL OIL BLEND

Use this combination of essential oils in diffusers or oil burners for an out-of-this-world room fragrance.

6 drops **JASMINE** essential oil
6 drops **LEMON** essential oil
6 drops **SANDALWOOD** essential oil
Small **DROPPER BOTTLE**

Add all the oils to a small clean dropper bottle and store in a cool, dark place.

* Alternatively, combine with fractionated coconut oil in a roller-ball vial for a mood-lifting fragrance.

UNICORN SUGAR SCRUB

1 cup granulated **SUGAR**
3 small glass **BOWLS**
½ cup **COCONUT OIL**, plus extra if needed
⅛ tsp each **MICA POWDER PIGMENT** in pink, blue
   and purple
HOLOGRAPHIC cosmetic-grade biodegradable
   BODY GLITTER* (optional)
2-3 drops each of **ROSE**, **BLUE LOTUS** and
   LAVENDER essential oils
Large **GLASS JAR** with a screw-top lid

Divide the sugar into three glass bowls. Add a
different mica powder colour to each one and mix.
Add in a pinch of glitter. Slowly add a third of the
coconut oil and a different essential oil to each bowl
and mix. Layer the colours in the jar and top with
glitter and the lid.

*Choose the eco-friendly non-toxic variety with mica
and agar (seaweed) for use in soap-making.

CHAPTER

Four

Unicorn Friendship

The unicorn is a friend to all the animals in the forest – no one is too insignificant for their attention.

Here's how to spread some unicorn kindness, gratitude, love and gentleness to your social circle and beyond.

"Life's not easy
for unicorns,
you know. We're a
dying breed."

MEG CALBOT,
TWITTER, JANUARY 30, 2014

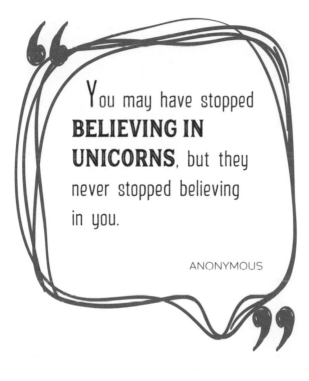

"You may have stopped **BELIEVING IN UNICORNS**, but they never stopped believing in you.

ANONYMOUS

Are You a Unicorn?

Identity unicorn-ness in yourself and others
with these 10 telltale signs.

1. YOU HAVE BOUNDLESS ENERGY
and tend to dance, prance or sprint rather than
sit still.

2. YOU ARE A LOYAL FRIEND – you like to do things
your way but you're always there for your pals.

3. YOU LIKE TO DRESS UP, show off your style and
are drawn to anything that sparkles: glitter, sequins,
metallics, lurex.

4. YOUR INNATE FABULOUSNESS MAKES YOU

THE CENTRE OF ATTENTION. People are drawn to you but they must beware: you are apt to suddenly shy away and disappear (probably onto something else more entertaining).

5. You are **OFTEN HARD TO CATCH** in romantic relationships.

6. YOU TAKE THE ROAD LESS TRODDEN.
The sheep go one way, and you go the other!

7. YOU DON'T HAVE A FAVOURITE COLOUR – all colours of the rainbow are equally extraordinary.

8. Sweets are your favourite food.

9. You look at the **SUNNY SIDE** of life.

10. YOU KNOW YOUR VALUE and protect it.

Unicorns can't fly.
I can't fly.
Therefore I am
a unicorn.

ANONYMOUS

Unicorn Astrology

In Celtic astrology, those born between 8 July and 4 August are under the Unicorn sign. These people are noted for being natural healers and nurturers. Trustworthy, they have a regal presence and make good leaders and problem-solvers. They follow through on action with intelligence and imagination.

Finding Your Unicorn
BFF

How do you find your unicorn friend – the one that you've always dreamed of, the one that *gets* you, your *person*? The most unlikely person might turn out to be the one that you bond with, so don't discount your opposite. It's often not about your common interests, social circles or the way you dress alike; it's about shared values and bonding over something simple – like a love for unicorns!

AFFIRMATION:
My Friendships Thrive

I attract positive friends who are loyal, inspiring and
motivating. They are real, honest and supportive.
Every day is an opportunity to meet someone new
and grow my friendship circle.

Acts of Kindness

Unicorns help others – they are the ones ensuring the animals of the forest have clean water after all!

Think of some kindnesses you can do for your friends, then cast the net wider and do something for someone you don't know well.

Feel brave, reach out and try something nice for a stranger.

Be Polite,
Be Gracious

A beautiful person shines from within. Foster that innate unicorn grace by practising kindness and politeness. Show a generosity of spirit toward others and avoid judging them (or yourself). Lend a helping hand. Caring for others will light you up inside.

AFFIRMATION:
I Attract Love

I am worthy of love and trust
in my relationships.
I am grateful for all who love
and care for me.

HOW TO BE A
SUPPORTIVE FRIEND

Friends are at the frontline and may notice things
that family or colleagues don't. Here are some ways
to be a caring pal when the going gets tough.

NOTICE: Be aware of any changes you see, such as
turning down invitations, avoiding things they usually
like and any mood changes.

CHECK IN: Find time for your people. Make sure you're asking questions about their life and feelings. Ask them what they need.

LISTEN: Give them the space to open up. Don't talk over them, and don't pressurize. Instead of trying to "fix" things, let them come to their own decisions.

LAUGH: Find the humour or absurdity in the situation and share the giggles.

TELL THE TRUTH: Be willing to be honest even if it's something they may not want to hear. The delivery of the message is important, so practise how you will frame it.

SHOW UP: Be there. Don't disappear.

Unicorn Crystals

Both crystals and unicorns are of the earth, and both also transcend the earthly plane to inhabit the heavenly. Here are the gemstones most associated with the unicorn that will help you tap into its purifying, healing and intuitive properties to mend yourself and relationships.

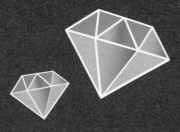

CHARGE YOUR CRYSTAL

Before working with a crystal, charge it in sunlight or moonlight and cleanse it in running water (see also page 77).

SET YOUR INTENTION

Holding the crystal in your right hand, set the intention to align with unicorn magic and think of the problem you need help with. Carry the crystal, wear it, sleep with it under your pillow or place it on an altar.

AMETHYST: A purple quartz with high spiritual vibration. Good for stress relief, sleep, dreams and physical healing.

 APOPHYLLITE: A bright white stone that aids astral and transdimensional travel. It is a spiritually strong stone with a high vibration.

 AQUAMARINE: Turquoise with water associations, it is purifying, detoxifying and aids clarity and communication.

 LARIMAR: A pale blue stone that brings joy, playfulness and optimism. It is helpful for dissolving fear and calming nervous energy.

AFFIRMATION:
Pure Thoughts

I ask my unicorn for protection
from evil intentions and toxic
thoughts, from wherever and
whomever they may arise.

Keep my mood positive, my heart
joyful and my mind and actions
pure and noble.

LEPIDOLITE: A sparkly lavender stone, excellent for attracting friendship and true love.

PERIDOT: A yellow-green gem reminiscent of summer grass, herbs, sunny days frolicking in fields. Attuned to nature, it is wonderful for grounding, health and confidence, and protection against darkness.

 ROSE QUARTZ: A pretty pink crystal that's very popular, it is associated with the heart, making it good for building relationships and giving and receiving love.

 WHITE QUARTZ: A white or clear crystal that acts as an energy amplifier for other stones and a purifier. The most important unicorn crystal, it is good for healing, removing blockages, and turning negative to positive.

Rose Quartz for Mending Fences

To heal rifts between friends or lovers, use rose quartz, which is **GREAT FOR BONDING AND BUILDING RELATIONSHIPS**. The crystal will also help disperse feelings of suspicion or resentment.

Place rose quartz in rooms that have discord and re-charge it once a week, clearing the room with a sage smudge stick in between. **THE ROOM SHOULD FEEL LIGHTER, AND BONDS BECOME RESTORED.**

Lepidolite for Letting Go

If you need to free yourself from a toxic relationship, this crystal can help gently nudge you to overcome emotional and mental dependencies and encourage self-love and self-trust. **IT WILL HELP RELIEVE THE PAIN OF A BAD SITUATION** and stabilize emotions.

Wear the stone next to your skin, as close as possible, so that it can help **REPEL THE TOXIC INFLUENCE AND STRENGTHEN YOUR SOUL.** This is not an easy relationship to exit and let go, so you may also want to combine it with amethyst which helps with addictions and healing.

UNICORN LOVE SPELL

The unicorn is associated with everlasting love
between soulmates, so use this spell to find yours.

Collect rose petals and take them to fast-flowing
water, such as a stream or waterfall. If you don't
have access to a natural site, seek out a fountain in
a park or use running tap water in your home.

Now visualize the qualities of your ideal partner –
it is best if you focus on the personality rather than
the physical appearance.
Keep a pure mind and intention.

Repeat:

**"WITH UNICORN MAGIC, PLEASE GRANT MY WISH AND
SEND ME MY LOVE AS I SEND THESE PETALS TO YOU."**

Then send the rose petals on the water to
the unicorn.

136

"Let us *only hate hatred*, **AND ONCE GIVE LOVE A PLAY,** we will fall in **LOVE** with a **UNICORN**."

HERMAN MELVILLE,
MARDI: AND A VOYAGE THITHER (1849)

YOUR UNICORN NAME

Take the first letter of your first name and match it to the names below to find your unicorn name.

For the surname, add together the day and month you were born, and keep adding until you get one digit.

For example, **25 DECEMBER WORKS OUT AS: 25 +12 = 37 AND 3+7 = 10 SO 1+0 = 1**

A Aurora

B Bella

C Crystal

D Daffy

E Elderberry

F Fluffy

G Gracie

H Hippy

I Ivy

J Jewel

K Kissie

L Larissa

M Merryweather

N Nellie

O Olena

P Pixie

Q Queenie

R Ruby

S Stormy

T Twinkle

U Unna

V Violet

W Willow

X Xeni

Y Yo-yo

Z Zelda

1 Moonbeam

2 Starburst

3 Razzle Dazzle

4 Bubbles

5 Firefly

6 Buttercup

7 Twilight

8 Rainbow

9 Bluebell

"Always be yourself, unless you can be a unicorn. Then, always be a unicorn."

ANONYMOUS

CHAPTER
Five

Unicorns at Play

Happiness, frolicking and playfulness are intrinsic characteristics of the unicorn, so get your joy on with these creative ideas for exploring fun and games.

I would compete in unicorn back riding! Why? Because we are from the same fairytale.

SASHA PIVOVAROVA,
AS SEEN ON
TWITTER

142

"Everything today has been
HEAVY and **BROWN**.
Bring me a *unicorn to ride*
about the town."

ANNE MORROW LINDBERGH,
BRING ME A UNICORN (1973)

The 8 Benefits of Play Time

No matter how old, or what creature, you are, play is essential to mental health and personal self-development. The old adage, "All work and no play makes Jack a dull boy", couldn't be more true.

1. INCREASES BRAIN FUNCTION.
Puzzles and strategic games like chess can improve memory and enhance problem-solving.

2. RELIEVES STRESS.
Play can trigger the release of endorphins, the feel-good hormone.

3. BOOSTS CREATIVITY.
Playing stimulates imagination and expands skills.

4. SUPERCHARGES LEARNING.
New skills are easier to learn when the instruction
is playful and relaxed.

5. CONNECTS YOU TO OTHERS and the world.
Participating in a shared event fosters intimacy,
bonding and trust, and opens you to other
perspectives.

6. MAKES YOU MORE PRODUCTIVE.
Play can boost energy and prevent burnout.

7. IMPROVES SOCIAL SKILLS.
Play van build relationships and increases
your network.

8. ENCOURAGES TEAM BUILDING.
Co-operation and collaboration are
essential in play.

145

"Imagine life as a game in which you are juggling some five balls in the air. You name them – work, family, health, friends and spirit – and you're keeping all of these in the air. You will soon understand that ***work is a rubber ball. If you drop it, it will bounce back.*** But the other four balls – **FAMILY, HEALTH, FRIENDS** and **SPIRIT** – are made of glass. If you drop one of these, they will be irrevocably scuffed, marked, nicked, damaged or even shattered."

BRIAN DYSON,
FORMER COO OF COCA-COLA

Time Out for Control Freaks

You schedule your whole work week, right? So why aren't you scheduling your entertainment? Book in fun for after work and weekend gallery visits, barbecues, sports events, cultural outings and even those walks in the park with friends.

* If you are not a control freak or workaholic, you probably already know how to manage your free time perfectly well.

Work-Play Balance

Here are some ideas to get more time into your life to relax, play and engage with the world without a goal or deadline as the objective.

★ Use unscheduled time to be creative, to daydream, reflect and decompress.

★ Be "in the moment". Try to focus on and appreciate what is happening right now.

★ Try new things and embrace the unexpected. If you see an opening for fun, take it; never turn it down.

★ Decide what fun means for you. Write a list of the things that bring you unadulterated joy now or in the past, and then list ways you can make those things happen regularly.

★ Set a minimum on fun times. If you are disciplined enough to exercise 30 minutes a day, you can certainly schedule in 30 minutes to have fun.

★ Create a play cupboard, drawer or box that contains games, jigsaw puzzles, colouring books, journals, juggling balls. Computer games are not included!

★ Have a kitchen disco for one. Dance like nobody is watching. Just two songs will lift your spirits, guaranteed.

★ Go people-watching on your lunch break. Real life is so fascinating!

★ Talk to strangers. Stop rushing around; strike up a conversation at your local coffee shop, café or bus stop.

★ Make your exercise goals feel like play. Try an unusual (for you) exercise class. Join a sports team. Try out a trampoline. Hop, skip and jump.

Rainbow Spotting

We all need **MORE** rainbows in our life.
Unfortunately, we can't conjure at will, but here are
the different types to look for.

**SOME SEE RAINBOWS AS A BRIDGE BETWEEN HEAVEN
AND EARTH OR LIFE AND DEATH**, but all cultures
consider them a sign of good luck.

SINGLE RAINBOW:
Everyone's seen these, the most common
type is called a primary rainbow.

DOUBLE RAINBOW:

This occurs when two or more rainbows appear in the sky at the same time. There is usually a primary with one or more "ghosts".

MONOCHROME RAINBOW:

When sunlight is travelling the farthest away through the atmosphere at either sunrise or sunset it can result in a rare and striking solidly red rainbow.

TWINNED RAINBOW:

Two rainbows form from a single
base point, splitting partway along
the arc.

PASTEL RAINBOW:

Supernumerary rainbows take place as
an extra band within a primary rainbow
(known as the stacker rainbow) or as an
additional rainbow right outside of the first.

REFLECTED RAINBOW: These appear in bodies of water below the horizon, commonly in puddles and birdbaths but also in large bodies of water.

FULL-CIRCLE RAINBOWS:
Only seen when you are on mountain tops, skyscrapers or in a plane, these are full rather than semi-circles.

RAINBOW WHEELS:
Dense rain or cloud create dark
shadows across a rainbow, making it look
like a wagon wheel.

FOGBOWS:
Caused when sunlight passes through
fog over water, they are typically
red, white and blue.

MOONBOWS:

Fainter and much more rare than the daytime version, these are caused by light reflected from moonlight.

SNOWBOWS:

A white or pale yellow colour, this circular 'bow can occur as a result of light striking snowflakes or ice crystals.

155

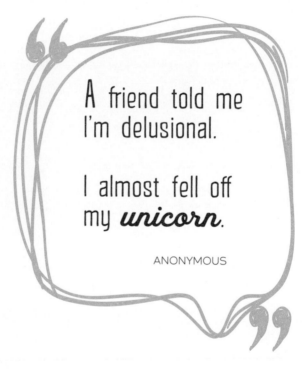

A friend told me
I'm delusional.

I almost fell off
my *unicorn*.

ANONYMOUS

Magic Fairy Ring

A faery ring is a circle of mushrooms growing naturally
in a glade or forest, but here you can create one as
a magical portal to your unicorn encounters.
Even if your unicorn doesn't turn up, another mystical
being is sure to!

★ **SMOOTH PEBBLES** or **STONES**
★ **CRYSTAL GLASS VESSELS** – fleamarket finds or odd
   pieces you've collected
★ String of **FAIRY LIGHTS** (battery-operated)

In the evening hours, find a spot outside that feels
magical to you. Set up your crystal pieces evenly
spaced in a circle, upending any bowls or glasses so
they appear like the curved tops of mushrooms and
toadstools. Run your fairy lights around the circle to
light up the crystals.

Turn on the lights and wait for your unicorn to arrive.
Be prepared for other visitors.

Explore Your Creativity

Even if you don't have a talent for drawing or painting, you can create collages of unicorn images or try sculpting with clay. Write some unicorn stories and poems of your own – create your own fairy tales and myths – and take off into the land of imagination.

AFFIRMATION:
My Ideas
Are Worthwhile

My creativity has purpose.
There is always a place in the
world for what I dream, imagine,
make and create.

UNICORN JOURNALING

To **STIMULATE YOUR IMAGINATION** and get your creative juices flowing, create a unicorn journal for all your *stories*, *dreams* and *thoughts*. Use colourful pens, glitter markers, stickers, glue-on **SPARKLES** and **STARS** to decorate the pages. Assign different colours to your moods and days of the week to track them in bullet-journal diary pages. To get you started, list the questions below and answer them.

WHAT DO YOU FIND OVER THE RAINBOW?

TODAY I SAW SOMETHING RARE AND SPECIAL. IT WAS...

If I had a magical power, it would be:

The last crazy fun thing I did was...

THE NEXT CRAZY FUN THING I WANT TO DO IS...

A UNICORN'S HOME IS FILLED WITH:

I'm taking a unicorn on holiday. We are going to:

161

"*Dreams*
are the **PLAYGROUND** of
UNICORNS."

ANONYMOUS

Unicorn Dreams

Dreams about unicorns are positive events and foretell good fortune. And in life, it is said that unicorns only appear in dreams to those who are true and honest.

A UNICORN RUNNING AWAY FROM YOU:
This represents a loss of innocence or broken trust. It may mean you are mourning your youthful, happy-go-lucky spirit.

UNICORN COMPANION: Get ready for an astral journey or out-of-body experience; the unicorn is your protector and guide through different dimensions and realms.

BABY UNICORN: If you have children, this indicates that you are a good parent or carer, or there is a child in your life who looks up to you. There may be a child in your future, or a new beginning of some kind.

FLYING UNICORN: Something new and exciting is about to happen, such as a marriage or trip to an exotic location.

RIDING A UNICORN: You are tired on your journey through life but you are being supported. You will get there, and overcome any obstacles, if not solely by your own steam.

TALKING UNICORN: Listen to the words – they are important! Unicorns are usually silent and prefer to communicate through symbols and actions.

Reach for the Stars!

To gallop towards your goal with the speed of a unicorn, cultivate emotional attachment to your dream. Use visualizations to maintain your motivation – see yourself taking the steps to achieve them, and make sure those steps are interesting enough to keep you engaged, urgent enough for you to feel time-committed to them and life-enhancing enough to result in a better future.

AFFIRMATION:
My Dreams
Can Become Reality

I AM PROUD of the person
I am today, and the person I will
be tomorrow.

CHAPTER
Six

Unicorn Charge

Channel unicorn energy
to supercharge your happiness,
positivity and confidence.

Learn how to say no powerfully,
to recognize toxicity and
inequality, and to stand up for
yourself and others.

"The unicorn, *through its intemperance* and not knowing how to control itself, for the love it bears to fair maidens **FORGETS ITS FEROCITY AND WILDNESS**; and laying aside all fear it will go up to a seated damsel and go to sleep in her lap, and **THUS THE HUNTERS TAKE IT.**"

LEONARDO DA VINCI,
THE NOTEBOOKS OF LEONARDO DA VINCI
(RICHTER, 1888)

"I DON'T WANT ANY UNICORNS BEHIND FENCES."

HARUKI MURAKAMI,
*HARD-BOILED WONDERLAND AND THE
END OF THE WORLD* (2010)

Vulnerabilities Are Your Secret Weapon

In a June 2010 TEDx Talk, psychologist Brené Brown said that authenticity is an essential part of developing meaningful relationships. When people show up, with all their vulnerabilities, it allows them to truly connect with and feel close to others; when they betray their true selves, they feel isolated and alone.

Sometimes you don't have all the answers and you have doubts. Far from being negatives, these all reveal that you are operating outside your comfort level and taking calculated risks, which is the only way to grow.

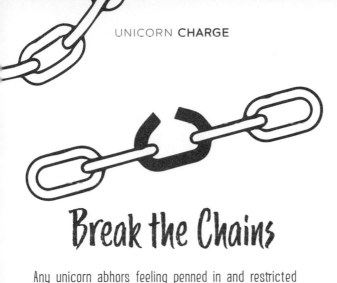

Break the Chains

Any unicorn abhors feeling penned in and restricted
– it goes against their free-spirit nature! If you are
chomping at the bit or feeling suffocated, say, at
work or in a relationship, first look at what's actually
holding you back.

Is it really someone or something else, or is it
you? Identify your feelings and address
any fears.

Let Your Unicorn Be Heard

Show your strength and speak up. If you have trouble voicing your opinions, connect with your passion, which will drive your argument and compel you to give voice. Don't forget to read the room – the most charismatic speakers always know when they've got their audience in the palm of their hand.

"

Poetry is news
BROUGHT TO THE MOUNTAINS
by a **UNICORN** and an
ECHO.

CZESŁAW MIŁOSZ,
*"INCANTATION", COLLECTED POEMS
1931–1987* (1988)

"

Being Persuasive

PASSION, **LOGIC** and *perception* – all
great unicorn traits – go far but sometimes they are
not enough to get others onside.

A study by the University of Leicester found that
**"THE SINGLE SIGNIFICANT
BEHAVIOURAL DIFFERENCE BETWEEN
PERSUADERS AND PERSUADEES WAS IN
THE EXPRESSION OF CONFIDENCE."**

Make your option beneficial and easy for others.
The less anyone has to do to get excellent results
will always be the preferred route.

Peacemaking Powers

Able to detect and judge **GOOD** and **EVIL**, the unicorn makes a fair and just mediator.

Try to see the whole picture and look at the problem and not the people or their attitudes. As all unicorns know, *speak judiciously* – how you deliver your message weighs with as much importance as the message in issues of conflict.

Defend Your Cause

Unicorns are formidable opponents. Channel your **POWER TO PROTEST** for the **CHANGE YOU WANT TO SEE IN THE WORLD.** Whether you are championing women's or LGBTQ+ rights, demonstrating for climate change or just passionate about supporting your local food drive, don't be afraid to **VOICE YOUR OPINIONS** and present your passion.

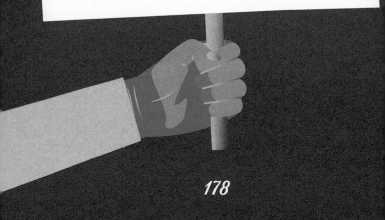

Say "No"

You would think it would be easy, but **THIS ONE WORD IS SO HARD TO SAY AND YET SO POWERFUL.** For people-pleasers it's especially difficult, but learning to refuse establishes and communicates your personal boundaries and limits, which in turn makes you stronger. Here are three tips.

★ **DON'T APOLOGIZE**, stall or try to couch it in polite language. Just say no.

★ **IDENTIFY PEOPLE'S AGENDAS**, tactics and tricks of coercion.

★ **STAND FIRM** and put your needs and priorities first. This is your life; you get to choose.

Quick Confidence Booster

When you feel unsure of yourself and lacking in self-belief, ignite the fire within by adapting the power pose by standing in the "wonder woman" stance. If this doesn't work for you, mentally re-play a time when you felt super-confident and try to encompass those feelings.

AFFIRMATION:
Happiness

I give and allow myself happiness in every moment and I follow my joy. Happiness is my true nature.

Ride the Unicorn

Embrace your inner insanity and don't hide the crazy. Some of the most important inventors, artists and leaders of all time were thought to be mad. Take a few moments each day to imagine the unimaginable and write down some "what ifs", such as "What would life be like if we could travel anywhere in the world in an hour?"

"*You are a f***ing unicorn* and all this time, you have been trying to be a horse. You very carefully hid your horn every time you stepped in the room ... **WHEN YOU HIDE WHO YOU ARE**, **TRULY**, MADLY, *deeply*, at the core of your being and try to fit into some other idea of you, you start to dull; **YOU SHINE LESS**."

BRYONIE WISE,
ELEPHANTJOURNAL.COM, DECEMBER 22, 2012

183

Steps to Self-love

1. **STOP COMPARING YOURSELF TO OTHERS.** There is only one you, and no one can compare!

2. **SHIFT FROM MAKING OTHERS HAPPY** to making yourself happy.

3. **IT'S OK TO MAKE MISTAKES.** Forgive yourself, learn from it and move on.

4. **YOUR VALUE DOESN'T LIE IN YOUR LOOKS.**

5. **SAY GOODBYE TO TOXIC PEOPLE** and situations.

6. **FEEL YOUR FEARS.** Identify and acknowledge them; don't ignore them.

7. **SPEAK YOUR MIND.** The more you exercise this, the stronger you get.

8. **ROW YOUR OWN BOAT.** You're not in a race and you get to decide how fast or slow you want to go.

Be Who You Came Here to Be

The greatest adventure in life is discovering who you are, what you want, what you like and how you want to live the one precious life you are given on this wild and weird planet. In his book *The Self Under Seige*, Dr Robert Firestone suggests that it is essential to break with your automatic assumptions about happiness and success, and develop your own values, ideals and beliefs distinct from your family and culture, in order to manifest your unique personhood.

"Make your life story *so amazing* that unicorns have trouble believing it is true."

KAREN SALMANSOHN,
PARADE, APRIL 2, 2021

187

AFFIRMATION:
Positivity

I breathe in energy and love.
I exhale negativity and self-doubt.
I create positive energy.

THE POWER OF POSITIVE THOUGHTS

LOOK ON THE BRIGHT SIDE OF LIFE.

Researchers at Kings College, London, in 2016 found that the happiest people owed their success to optimism. One easy way to increase your positivity is to replace the words you use in conversation and self-talk.

AVOID: "WORRIED", "SCARED", "UPSET", "TIRED", "BORED", "NOT", "NEVER", and "CAN'T" and "THE PROBLEM IS..."

USE: "EXCITED", "HAPPY", "PEACEFUL", "CALM", "LOVING", "ENTHUSIASTIC" and "WARM".

189

8 Ways to Build Resilience

Unicorns never die and they never give up. When faced with a challenge or penned in a corner, they consistently knock it out of the park. Here's how.

1. **RELAX.** Being physically calm will encourage mental calmness.

2. **PRACTISE MINDFULNESS.** Be aware of any negative thought patterns.

3. **REFRAME.** Change the way you view mistakes or setbacks.

4. **LEARN FROM FAILURE.** The most transformative life changes happen as a result of "failures".

5. CONSIDER YOUR REACTION. Logically think about your actions and modify your reactions.

6. MATCH YOUR GOALS TO YOUR VALUES.
If you're trying to achieve something you don't believe in, it will never work.

7. CONSIDER YOUR PERSPECTIVE.
Look at things from the "devil's advocate" point of view.

8. BE FLEXIBLE. Everything is in a state of flux – learn to adapt to shifting sands.

"Here's to the **CRAZY** ones, the *misfits*, the **REBELS**, the troublemakers, the round pegs in the square holes... *the ones who see things differently* – they're not fond of rules..."

APPLE MAC'S "THINK DIFFERENT" CAMPAIGN (1997)